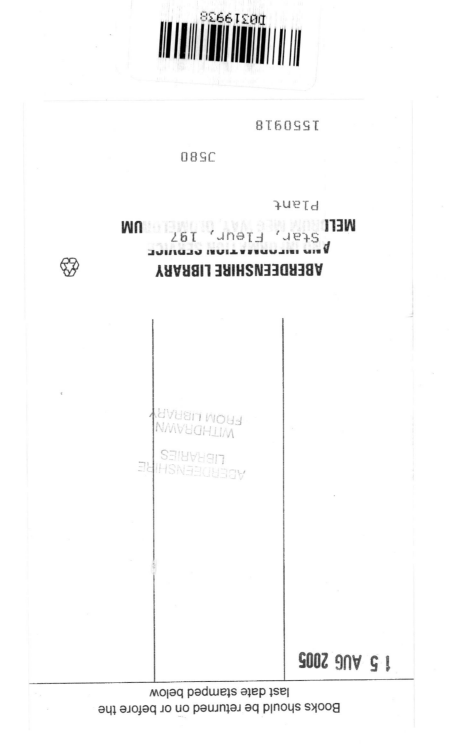

DK Eye Wonder

Plant

LONDON, NEW YORK, MUNICH,
MELBOURNE, and DELHI

Written and edited by Fleur Star
Designed by Janet Allis

Publishing manager Sue Leonard
Managing art editor Clare Shedden
Jacket design Chris Drew
Picture researcher Sarah Pownall
Production Luca Bazzoli
DTP Designer Almudena Díaz
Consultant Sandra Bell

First published
Dorlin
80 Stran

2 4 6 8 10 9 7 5 3 1

Copyright © 2005 Dorling Kindersley Limited, London

A CIP catalogue record for this book
is available from the British Library.

ISBN 1-4053-0598-3

Colour reproduction by Colourscan, Singapore
Printed and bound in Italy by L.E.G.O.

see our complete
catalogue at
www.dk.com

Contents

What is a plant?

Hibiscus plant

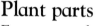

Anthers

Flower bud

Flower

Leaf bud

Stalk

Leaf

Life on Earth is divided into plants, animals, and fungi. There are thought to be about 400,000 species of plants in the world. The first plants – algae, which live in water – appeared about 3 billion years ago.

Plant parts

Every part of a plant has a job to do. Leaves make food, the stem carries water, and flowers make seeds. All flowering plants have the same basic make-up, even if they look quite different.

Woody stem

Roots divide to hold the plant in the ground.

Roots

Sunlight *Air* *Water*

Minerals from soil

Plant needs

A plant needs four things to survive: sunlight, water, minerals, and air. Minerals come from the soil, while air provides the gases for breathing and photosynthesis (making food).

4

First flowers

Ancient fossils show that some of the first flowers looked very much like magnolias. They share features that not all plants have, such as having many anthers.

Lichen growing on trees is usually grey, green, or yellow.

Is it a plant?

Lichen, seen here growing on rotten trees, is a partnership of algae and fungi. Unlike algae, lichen and fungi are not plants because they do not make their own food through photosynthesis.

First plants

Non-flowering plants, such as ferns and mosses, are among the oldest plants in the world. About 300 million years ago great forests of them covered the land.

Ferns and mosses do not have seeds, but reproduce from spores.

Grow up!

A seed is a pocket-sized plant. It contains everything that a plant has: leaves, stems, and roots, plus food, or nutrients, for the time the plant is inside the seed. Some seeds can lie around for years waiting for the right conditions to grow.

Inside story

To start growing, a seed needs air, water, and the right temperature. The seed absorbs air and water, which makes it swell and split. Then the first root breaks through.

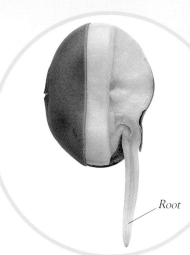

Root

The first shoot is made up of the leaves and stem.

Plant words

Germinate When a seed starts growing into a plant.

Root The part of a plant that grows underground and absorbs water and nutrients.

Shoot Any part of a plant that grows above ground, such as the stem or leaves.

Reach for the Sun

As soon as the leaves are out, they begin to catch sunlight to make food. Now the plant has grown, the seed will shrivel because it is no longer needed.

Cracking up

Young plants are surprisingly strong. They can force their way up through rocks, tarmac and cracks in the pavement. You might be able to find some growing through your garden path!

Roots keep the plant fixed firmly in the ground.

Taking root

Roots spread out underground to absorb water and nutrients from the earth. They are covered in hairs to take in as much water as possible.

7

Putting down roots

Roots do two things: they anchor plants and keep them secure, and they absorb water and food. Some roots have weird and wonderful ways of doing this!

Far out

Roots can only grow where there is water. Tree roots near the surface grow outwards, up to four times the width of the tree. Other roots can dig down deep enough to break through sewers.

Stuck in the mud

Mangroves live in swamps. Their huge prop roots support the stems to stop them being washed away. The tangled roots also trap mud, which has nutrients for the tree.

Storage system

Not everything underground is a root. Bulbs are food storage systems that contain the leaves and stems of new plants. When the plant grows, the roots descend.

Big butts

When trees grow in shallow soil, such as in rainforests, their roots might grow above the surface of the ground. These are buttress roots, which keep the tree stable. Some can grow to 4.5 m (15 ft) tall.

GRASS ROOTS

In 1937, an American scientist called Howard Dittmer studied the roots of a rye grass plant. The plant was just 50 cm (20 in) tall, and had 80 shoots. But it had more than 620 km (380 miles) of roots! They could cover an area of 237 sq m (2,554 sq ft), enough to carpet a large house. And this doesn't include the 14 billion root hairs!

Leaf it out

All leaves are made up of a blade on a stalk, but each different kind has it own shape, colour, and way of growing. This is because plants have leaves that suit the environment in which they grow.

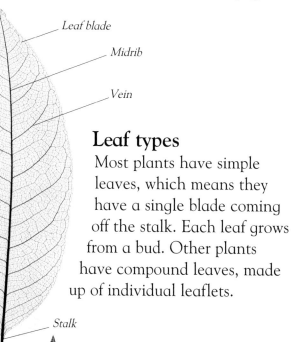

Simple

Leaf blade

Midrib

Vein

Leaf types
Most plants have simple leaves, which means they have a single blade coming off the stalk. Each leaf grows from a bud. Other plants have compound leaves, made up of individual leaflets.

Stalk

Palmate leaves look like hands. They can be simple or compound, like this horse chestnut.

Many pine trees grow in cold places. Their needles are thin and pointed to shake off snow.

A variegated leaf has spots of different colours, which come from chemicals inside the leaf.

Palmate

Needles

Variegated

What a drip

Leaves cannot absorb water, so they have drainage systems to stop them drowning. Water collects in ridges and runs off a "drip-tip" on the end of the leaf.

Some leaves turn red from waste products stored inside.

Drip-tip

Changing colour

Leaves get their green colour from chlorophyll, which they use to make food. When the leaves rest in the autumn, the chlorophyll fades away, revealing the reds and yellows of other chemicals in the leaf.

The leaflets of a compound leaf grow straight from the stalk, not from buds.

Compound

The "leaves" of wild asparagus are really feathery stems that can stand up to gales.

Feathery

11

Food factories

Plants are unique – they are the only living things that make their own food. This process is called photosynthesis, which can only happen in the daytime because it uses sunlight.

Sunlight

Carbon dioxide

Plants lose water and gases from their leaves.

What's cooking?

Leaves take in sunlight, carbon dioxide (CO_2) from the air, and water from the roots and mix them together using chlorophyll. This recipe makes glucose, a type of sugary plant food, and oxygen.

Oxygen

Air holes

The carbon dioxide used in photosynthesis is taken in through stomata, tiny holes on the surface of every leaf. They also "breathe out" any extra oxygen that the plant does not use for respiration.

Open stomata

Leaf words

Photosynthesis The unique way plants make their own food.

Respiration How living things turn food into energy.

Chlorophyll A chemical found inside leaves that is used for photosynthesis.

Going green

This close-up of a leaf shows green dots inside the cells. These are the stores of chlorophyll, and they give leaves their green colour.

Carbon dioxide

Spare CO₂ that has not been used for making food is released back into the air.

Energy source

Like all living things, plants get energy from food. This is called respiration. Plants use oxygen to turn food into energy, which helps them to grow. The oxygen comes from the air or from photosynthesis.

Oxygen

Closed for the night

Respiration occurs 24 hours a day, but photosynthesis stops at night when there is no sun. Many plants close their stomata at night as they rest. Oxygen and CO_2 can still pass in and out of the leaf cells even though the stomata are shut.

Water

Closed stomata

Pollination

Watch a patch of flowers on a summer's day and you will soon see a bee or a butterfly. Many flowers need these insects for pollination (the transfer of pollen from plant to plant).

Normal light

Ultra-violet light

Take a close look

Pollination happens when pollen from one plant's anthers is carried to the stigma of another. The pollen then fertilizes an egg in the ovary, the first step to making a seed.

Landing lights

This flower looks plain yellow to us, but insects can see ultra-violet light. This shows up patterns on flowers called nectar guides. They point out exactly where the nectar is in the flower, leading insects straight to it.

Anther

Anther

Stigma

Style

Petal

Ovary

Pollination facts

- A honeybee may visit 10,000 flowers in one day.

- Bees account for 80 per cent of all insect pollination.

- Some plants rely on the same insect for pollination, others may be pollinated by several different insects.

The bee uses its proboscis to suck up nectar to take back to the hive.

A good dusting

When a bee lands on a flower, its body is dusted with pollen. It collects this pollen in pollen baskets on its back legs, but enough is left to pollinate other flowers.

Pollen

Magnified many times, pollen grains are differently shaped depending on their parent plant. Some have spiky casings.

The bee mixes pollen with nectar, making it sticky so it stays in the pollen baskets.

Busy as a bee

Bees pollinate many of the world's crops, from apples and pears to cucumbers and melons. They zip between the flowers at the dizzy speed of 24 kph (15 mph).

Flower partners

Just like you might prefer one drink to another, some animals will choose to drink nectar from certain plants. And these plants will try all sorts of tricks to attract their chosen pollinator.

Smelling right is as important as looking pretty.

Going batty
In the deserts of North America, long-nosed bats feed from century plants. The bat's thick fur picks up lots of pollen as it buries its head in the flower for a drink of nectar.

Bee mine
Bee orchids look and smell like female bees to attract male bees. There are around 130 types of bee orchid in Europe that impersonate different kinds of bees.

Perfect pairs

- A carpenter bee buzzes at the right pitch to shake loose the pollen of a gentian flower.

- The dead-horse arum stinks of rotting meat to attract blow-flies.

- Moths seek pale yellow or white flowers at night.

Fly-by feeder
Hummingbirds can access flowers that other birds cannot reach, because they are the only birds that can hover in mid-air. Flowers that want to attract birds are usually coloured red.

Lap it up

In New Zealand, flax plants provide a
tasty drink for geckos. As they climb up
the stem and drink from the flower, they
get pollen all over their chins.

*The yellow
pollen stains
the gecko's chin.*

Running wild

Tiny honey possums in
Australia clamber all over
the flowers of a banksia
plant to gather nectar.
Of course, they get covered
in pollen while doing so!

Going to seed

Flowering plants reproduce by making seeds, which happens after a plant has been pollinated. Seeds are valuable and need protecting, so a plant will grow fruit to cover the seeds.

From blossom to apple

An apple tree's white blossom appears in the spring. When the blossom is pollinated, it makes seeds. Then an apple grows from each blossom to protect the seeds. By autumn, the apple is fully grown and ready to eat!

Seeds

Sunflower seeds can be roasted and eaten in salads.

Seeds

Seed head

A sunflower is made up of lots of little flowers, each of which make a seed when it is pollinated. There are around 1,000 seeds inside just one sunflower head. Every seed is surrounded by its own case.

Wooden fruit

Not all fruit is edible: the fruit of pine trees are wooden cones. Pine trees take two years to make seeds, which are kept safe inside the cones. When the seeds are ready, the cones burst open. The seeds fall to the ground, where many will be eaten by forest animals and birds.

Seeds

Spores on underside of a fern leaf.

Scores of spores

Non-flowering plants do not have seeds. Ferns have spores instead, which can be seen on the underside of the leaves. When the spores are ripe, they fall off the leaf.

New potato plants sprouting.

Sprouting spuds

Have you ever seen an old, wrinkly potato? It probably has "eyes" – green buds that will grow into new plants. Potatoes are not seeds, but tubers, which are underground food stores for the plant.

Strawberries have seeds, but new plants grow more easily from runners.

19

Carried away

Plants spread their seeds so they can grow in new places. This is called seed dispersal. It gives the seeds a chance to find sunlight, water, and food that are not already being used by the parent plant or by other seeds.

The pod pushes the seeds forward.

A flying start
Impatiens are a group of garden plants sometimes called "touch-me-nots". Their seed pods are ready to burst at the slightest touch. Seeds are flung out, although they don't travel far.

Get stuck in
Have you ever let a pet dog run in fields? It might have come back with burrs in its fur. Burrs are seeds with sticky or spiky coats that grip animal fur, later falling off onto new ground.

SPIT OUT THE SEEDS
The Mediterranean squirting cucumber has a messy method of seed dispersal. As it grows, each cucumber fruit fills with slime until there's no more room. Then, suddenly... POP! The fruit bursts, comes off its stalk, and flies through the air like a rocket for 6 m (20 ft), spraying slime and seeds behind it.

Just passing through
Fruit is tasty and colourful to get animals to eat it. Animals swallow seeds with the fruit. When the seeds have passed through the animal, they are far away from the parent plant.

The wind will carry these seeds for many kilometres.

Propeller powered
Sycamore seeds are among the heaviest to ride on the wind. Their shape works like a helicopter rotor, spinning round in the breeze so the seeds travel further.

Blowing in the wind
A dandelion seed is so light it can be blown away by the wind, carried on its own fluffy white parachute. A dandelion is not one flower, but is made up of florets that each make a seed when pollinated. One plant can make up to 500 seeds.

Go with the flow
Coconuts may be one of the largest seeds, but they are hollow and light enough to float. This way they can travel across oceans, and they have been known to survive journeys of 1,600 km (1,000 miles).

On the menu

All life on Earth depends on plants. Even those animals that just eat meat, eat other animals who feed on plants. People have been growing plants for food for thousands of years.

Sweet seeds

Chocolate is made from the seeds of a cocoa tree. The white seeds inside the pods are dried and ground into cocoa powder, which actually tastes quite bitter.

A cereal success story

Wheat is the world's most widely-grown plant, found on every continent except Antarctica. It is a type of grass called a cereal, which means it has seeds that can be made into flour. This group also includes oats, maize, and rice.

Herbs and spices

A herb is any plant with a non-woody stem, but what cooks call herbs are leaves or flowers of certain, safe-to-eat plants. Spices, such as pepper, are made from ground seeds or bark.

Spoilt for choice

A vegetable is a plant or part of a plant that is grown to be eaten. This includes fruit, seeds, roots, and leaves, such as beans (seeds) and carrots (roots). But there is no one plant that we can eat every part of.

23

Plant protection

Plants have many ways to defend themselves from being trampled or eaten. Some have built-in protection, such as thorns. Other plants might form a partnership with animals. They can't run away from predators!

The tree's spiky thorns do not stop the giraffe from having a good chew.

Sharp taste
Ants live inside the thorns of acacia trees, safe from predators. In return, they protect the tree by biting the tongues of animals eating the tree.

Prickly customer

Woody thorns line the stems of brambles and roses. They can get tangled in animal fur and give a painful scratch to anyone that comes too near.

Nasty nettles

Stings are not like thorns. They are a type of hair that contain poison. When a predator brushes against the nettle, the sting stabs them, snaps off, and releases the poison. Ouch!

Water collects here and insects can't climb out.

Spines, called bracts, protect the flower.

Double defence

Teasels are well prepared for attack. Insects climbing up the stem will find spines, but if they head back down, they will drown in a leaf moat. This is the dip where two leaves meet, which fills with water when it rains.

Spot the plant

Hidden among the stones in African deserts are small, round plants. They have dull patterns that act as camouflage. You can see why they're called pebble plants.

Tree types

All trees fit into one of three categories, which are based on the shape of their leaves. They are broadleaved, needle-leaved, and palm.

Broadleaved trees have a variety of leaf shapes. Oak leaves are lobed, which means they have rounded points.

Growth rings

A tree grows by adding a layer of cells around its trunk. One layer is added every year. You can tell how old a tree was by counting the number of growth rings inside the trunk.

Out for the summer

Broadleaved trees have flat, broad leaves. Most trees of this kind are deciduous. This means their leaves die in the winter and fall off.

Small, tough leaves can stand up to the cold weather.

The world's biggest leaves belong to palm trees. Raffia palm leaves can grow to 20 m (65 ft).

Give us a hand

A palm tree's canopy – its branches and leaves – looks like a hand, with the leaves spreading out like fingers. There are more than 3000 species of palm, mostly found in tropical places.

Green all year

Needle-leaved trees, such as pines and firs, are known as coniferous because they make seeds inside cones. They are also called evergreens because they keep their leaves in winter.

Tree house

Look closely at a mature European oak tree and you will find an amazing array of animals making their homes there. For some, food is also provided in the form of acorns.

Nursery food
A female acorn weevil uses her long snout to drill into an acorn before laying her eggs inside. When they hatch, the babies, or larvae, feed on the acorn.

Bed and breakfast
An oak tree produces 90,000 acorns a year. They are eaten by forest animals, but wood pigeons are the greediest: they can stuff 70 acorns into their throat.

Going batty
Bats' favourite roosts are in dark, hidden places where they can shelter during the daytime. Hollows inside tree trunks and rotten boughs are ideal. In some countries, bats prefer to live in trees.

Tree house facts
The oak tree holds the European record for the most number of animals living in a tree. It is home to

- 30 species of birds
- 200 species of moths
- thousands of insects

Rabbit run
Down among the roots of the oak, there is a network of underground tunnels, which form a rabbit warren. The soil here is easy to dig.

Home to roost

Owls do not build nests in tree canopies like other birds, but roost inside the trunk. Living in a forest with other animals around means they can find lots of prey to eat.

Bark gallery

Bark beetles gnaw tunnels, called galleries, below the surface of the trunk. It is a safe place to lay eggs, but larvae can destroy a tree by eating its wood.

Muscling in

Not all plants create their own food. Some are parasites, living off the food other plants – called hosts – have made. Epiphytes are not so mean. They use other plants, but don't take their nutrients.

Going up in the world

Bromeliads are epiphytes. They grow on tree trunks and branches so they can be carried up to the sunlight as the tree grows. If these small plants stayed on the forest floor, they would die from lack of light.

Big stinker

The world's largest flower is a parasite. Rafflesia is 1 m (3 ft) wide and feeds off rainforest vines. It attracts pollinators with its stink of rotting meat.

Mistletoe roots are completely blended into the tree branch.

Branching out

Mistletoe is a lazy plant. It has leaves that can make their own food, but doesn't use them much. Instead, it sends roots down into its host's branches and steals the sap.

Deadly dodder

On the ground, dodder plant tendrils go hunting for food. They wrap around the stems of other plants and suck the life out of them.

Strangle hold

Strangler figs are not parasites – they live off debris found in the host tree. But as their roots descend the host's trunk, they block out the sunlight and the host dies.

The fig starts life as a seed landing on a branch, and sends down roots as it grows.

The roots keep the fig standing even after the host has rotted away.

Meat-eaters

Not all plants feed on sunlight and water alone – some add meat to their diet to give them extra nutrients. There are four main ways meat-eating, or carnivorous, plants catch their prey.

It's a trap!
Tiny hairs inside the leaves of a Venus fly trap can sense when an insect has landed. If two or more hairs are touched together... SNAP! It slams shut.

Digesting cells
When an insect has been caught, glands on the inside of the trap get to work. They release a kind of acid that starts to digest the insect.

The insect inside this Venus fly trap is being prepared for lunch.

Slippery pitch

The pitcher plant can catch loads of insects inside its huge leaves. The insects can't climb out of the waxy leaves, and they drown in the liquid at the bottom of the deep pit.

The pitcher's walls are thin so the plant can absorb the nutrients from the insects.

Watch out!

The rim of the pitcher is coloured to attract insects – and slippery so they fall in.

The sundew acts just like flypaper.

Meaty facts

● Most carnivorous plants live in marshy areas where the earth alone does not provide enough nutrients.

● The biggest carnivorous plant – a kind of pitcher – has vines up to 10 m (33 ft) long. It can catch frogs!

Sticky business

An unfortunate fly lands for a moment on a sundew fly trap... and remains stuck fast. The leaves are covered in sticky hairs that trap the insect, ready for eating later.

There is no way a fly can free itself from the many sticky hairs.

The leaf curls around the fly to bring it towards the digestion cells.

The bladder is full of hairs that sense prey.

Tiny trapdoors

When prey floats past this underwater bladderwort, the bladders on the leaves quickly open, like a mouth, sucking the insect inside. It takes one-thousandth of a second to trap the prey.

Any bits of fly that the plant doesn't digest are left stuck to the leaf.

Creepers and climbers

Climbing plants – also called creepers – grow by wrapping themselves around supports. They are strong and can push their way into all sorts of places, sometimes damaging the very thing that supports them.

Leaf climbers

Clematis plants use their leaves to climb. The leaf stalk twists around a thin support, such as a stem of another plant. The other plant does all the hard work of standing upright.

Curly tendrils on climbing plants

Reach out

This climbing plant has curly tendrils growing from its stem. These act like hands, reaching out for a surface to wrap around. Tendrils grow straight but curl up so they can pull the plant upright.

Champion climber

Stem climbers, such as morning
glory, can climb over anything.
They are able to wrap their stems
around larger objects than tendrils
or leaf stalks can, including
tree trunks.

can s t r - e - t - c h a long way.

Getting a grip

These strange-looking fingers
growing from ivy stems are roots.
They are slightly sticky and
can grip almost any surface.
It is easy for ivy to cover
whole houses, worming
its roots into the bricks.

Water worlds

All plant life started in the water with algae, the first plant family. Today, an incredible 85 per cent of plants live in the oceans. They have special features to help them survive in water.

Water of life

Seaweed is a type of algae. It does not have roots, but absorbs water and nutrients through its fronds. It needs to stay covered in water – if it gets washed ashore, it will die.

Some algae are so tiny, 25 million can fit in a teaspoon!

See the light

Just like land plants, algae needs sunlight to make food. Algae can be red, yellow, green, or brown; these colours detect sunlight at different depths in the sea.

Stuck on you

These slimy tubes are holdfasts. They keep a plant rooted in one place. But they are not actually roots because they do not absorb nutrients.

DON'T TRY THIS AT HOME

The leaves of the Amazon water lily can grow to 1.8 m (6 ft) across. As well as being large, they are surprisingly strong. This was discovered by Joseph Paxton, an English gardener, about 150 years ago. He noticed the ribs underneath the leaves and tested their strength... by asking his daughter to sit on a leaf in the middle of a pond!

Float on by

Floaters such as water hyacinths have roots that are the opposite of holdfasts. They are not anchored to the ground, but trail behind the plant as it swims along, picking up nutrients.

Through the surface

Emergent plants, such as lilies, are rooted in a pond or river bed, but grow tall to poke through the surface of the water. This enables them to reach the light.

On dry land

Water is hard to find in the desert, but when the rains come, the plants are ready. They can take in lots of water in a short time, and store water for a long time. Plants that store water in their leaves or stems are called succulents.

The word "cactus" comes from the Greek kaktos, which means "prickly plant".

WATER STORAGE

Many cactus stems look like they are creased. These deep ridges show clearly when the plant is dry. When the rains come, the ridges expand so the cactus has room to take in lots of water. Rather than having leaves, a cactus has spines growing from its stem. They protect the fat, juicy plant from being eaten by animals that are looking for a quick drink.

Is it dead or alive?

Not all plants store enough water to get through the dry season. Dried resurrection plants curl into a ball, pull up their roots from the ground, and get blown by the wind to a place where they may find water and come back to life.

A flash of colour

Deserts are not always dry. There is a short spring season that brings heavy rains. Plants that live here are ready to germinate and flower very quickly – the season lasts just three weeks.

Bottled water

This funny-looking tree is called a pachypodium, which means "thick foot". Its bottle-shaped trunk is fat and swollen with stored water.

Keep your hair on

The hairy white spines of these cacti reflect the strong heat of the desert sun. This built-in sunscreen stops the plant drying out.

It's full of water

Juicy, fleshy, waxy leaves are the sign of most succulents. This is where the plant stores its water. The waxy coating stops water evaporating from the leaves.

Cold climate

Welcome to the mountains. Plants that live here have developed ways to cope with cold temperatures, snow, high winds, and strong sunlight. From warm coats to heated buds, these plants know how to protect themselves.

A snug coat

Many cold-climate plants have small leaves, because large leaves lose heat more quickly. Edelweiss leaves are also covered in hairs, which act like a warm coat in the open mountains.

A miniature ice breaker

Some plants try to beat the weather by flowering early. Alpine snowbells lying under snow heat the tips of their buds. This melts the snow so they can push through to the surface to flower.

Don't sit on me!

Alpine plants grow low to the ground to avoid ferocious winds. Some, called cushion plants, even grow huddled together for warmth. They look like huge pillows scattered on the ground. Up to a million plants can grow in one clump.

A bad hair day?

Saussurea plants have taken the idea of a fur coat to the extreme. The pink fluff is not its flower, but hair on the leaves. On some plants hair reflects the harsh sunlight, stopping it from burning the plant.

Springtime is short, so flowers don't have much time for pollination.

I'm over here

Alpine flowers are brightly coloured and quite large. There are not many insects in this cold area, so the flowers need to show off in order to attract their pollinators.

Plant providers

Is your table made from wood, or are your clothes made from cotton? Plants provide us with lots of everyday items, from the houses in which we live to the pages of this book.

Spin a yarn

Linen is made from a plant called flax, one of the first plants grown by people just to be used. Flax fibres are spun to make threads, which are woven into material.

Bamboo bounty

Bamboo is possibly the most useful plant of all, and is especially popular in Asia. Its strong, tube-shaped stems have dozens of uses, from furniture and water pipes to hats.

Use it all up

This entire house has been made from palm trees. The trunk gives timber for the frame and walls, and the leaves are used as thatch. Palm fruit, coconut, is also used for food, milk, and oil. Even the hair on the coconut shell is turned into mats.

On a roll

Imagine a world with no paper. No books, boxes, or even tissues, which are all made from mashed-up wood chips. If you grew a tree to make the amount of paper you used every year, it would be 30 m (100 ft) tall.

42

A cork oak tree is stripped for its cork bark. It will take about seven years to regrow. Cork was first used by the ancient Greeks 2,500 years ago as bottle stoppers.

Strange but true

These weird and wonderful plants are some of the oldest or smelliest plants in the world. This is quite an achievement when there are over 400,000 species to choose from!

A late developer

Believe it or not, this 12 m- (40 ft-) tall plant is a herb! It holds the record for being the slowest-flowering plant. It takes 150 years to flower, but after all that effort, it dies.

It's one big stinker

The smelliest flower of all is the corpse flower, a kind of lily that grows in rainforests in Indonesia. Its "perfume" of rotting meat can be smelt a kilometre away.

Turn left at the tree

Giant sequoias are the world's biggest trees. In some Californian parks, the trees are so wide that they have roads cut though them.

Old and gnarled

The oldest tree thought to be still alive is a bristlecone pine. It is almost 5,000 years old, but, because they grow in dry places, even young ones look wrinkled!

Oh so rare

In the 1800s, the Lady's slipper orchid was picked almost to extinction. Just one plant was left in the wild. Fortunately, scientists have been able to use its seeds to plant more.

Strange facts

● There is one plant that grows so fast you can hear it creaking! Giant bamboo can grow 1 m (3 ft) each day.

● The biggest seed in the world is the coco-de-mer. It weighs up to 20 kg (45 lb), the same as a six-year-old girl.

Keep on twisting

The weirdest plant of all is found in the Namibian desert. It has just two leaves that are dry and woody, but they never stop growing so they end up all twisted.

Glossary

Here are the meanings of some words it is useful to know
when you are learning about plants.

Anther the part of a flower that makes pollen.

Blade the flat surface of a leaf, which is used to catch sunlight for photosynthesis.

Burr a seed with a sticky or spiky case.

Canopy the branches and leaves of a tree.

Carnivore an animal or plant that eats meat.

Chlorophyll the green chemical in a leaf that absorbs sunlight to make food.

Epiphyte a plant that grows on another plant, but does not take its food or water.

Floret a small flower that makes up part of a larger flower.

Flower the part of a plant that makes seeds and fruit.

Fruit the part of a plant that protects fertilized seeds.

Germinate when a seed starts to grow into a plant.

Glucose the sugary food a plant makes for itself during photosynthesis.

Leaf the part of a plant that makes food.

Leaflet a small leaf that is part of a compound leaf.

Minerals substances that are found naturally in soil, which a plant needs to grow.

Nectar sweet syrup that flowers make to attract pollinators.

Nectar guides patterns on flowers that guide insects towards the nectar.

Nutrients the useful bits found in food, which animals and plants need to stay healthy.

Ovary the part of a flower that houses the seeds.

Parasite a plant that takes the food and water of another plant.

Photosynthesis the way that a plant makes its own food, using sunlight, water, and carbon dioxide.

Pollen very fine grains that a plant uses to start reproduction.

Pollination the process of moving pollen from one flower to another in order to reproduce.

Predator an animal that hunts plants or other animals for food.

Proboscis the long nose of an insect, which can reach into flowers to suck up nectar.

Reproduction how a plant or animal makes another plant or animals, using seeds or eggs.

Respiration how living things turn food into energy, using oxygen.

Root the part of a plant that grows underground, anchoring the plant and taking in water and minerals.

Runner a plant stem that runs along the ground and grows new plants by sending out roots.

Seed a case that contains everything needed to grow a new plant, plus food.

Shoot any part of a plant that grows above the ground.

Species a group of animals or plants that share the same features, and can breed with each other.

Spore the "seed" of a non-flowering plant.

Stem usually the main part of a plant, on which leaves grow. Stems carry water and food around the plant.

Stigma the part of a flower that receives pollen during pollination.

Stomata tiny pores in a leaf that open to let gases pass in and out.

Succulent plants that store water in their leaves or stems.

Tendril the part of a stem that some climbing plants use to reach out for supports.

Tuber part of a root that has become a food store for the plant. It is usually lumpy.

Vegetable a plant or part of a plant that we can eat. Many vegetables are actually fruit.

Index

Acknowledgements

Dorling Kindersley would like to thank:
Janet Allis for additional artworks, Caroline Bingham for editorial assistance and Jacqueline Gooden for design assistance.

Picture credits

The publisher would like to thank the following for their kind permission to reproduce their photographs:

Key: a-above; c-centre; b-below; l-left; r-right; t-top

Alamy Images: Daniel Jenkins 21tl; David Boag 21br; David Wootton 30br; Jacques Jangoux 5br; Peter Haigh 45r. **Ardea.com:** Jason Mason 25ca. **Corbis:** Anders Ryman 42cra; Brian A Vikander 24l; Brian Knox; Papilio 40cr; Charles O'Rear 43; Craig Tuttle 27r, 40-41; Doug Wilson 26-27tc; Douglas Peebles 8l; Galen Rowell 36cr, 44l; Geray Sweeney 42tl; Hal Horwitz 31tc, 45cl; Kevin Schafer 31r; L. Clarke 12-13; Larry Lee Photography 11c; Lester Lefkowitz 42br; Marin Harvey; Gallo Images 4cr; Michael & Patricia Fogden 39r; Michael Pole 8c; Michael T. Sedam 18l; Paul Almasy 26-27c; Peter Johnson 45b; Ralph A. Clevenger 36l; Randy Wells 22cr; Reuters 44cr; Robert Holmes 45tl; Robert van der Hilst 22tl; Rocardo Azoury 30l; Sally A. Morgan/Ecoscene 19tl; Terry W. Eggers 26l; W. Perry Conway 32br. **Garden Picture Library:** Dennis Davis 41tl. **Garden World Images:** 1. **Getty Images:** Giel 20br; Simon Battensby 4cra; Steve Satushek 10-11; Stuart Dee 23. **ImageState:** Brand X Pictures 38. **Nature Picture Library Ltd:** Jason Smalley 28-29; Kevin J Keatley 29cl; Nigel Bean 28cl; Sharon Heald 39cl. **N.H.P.A.:** Daniel Heuclin 39tl, 39tc; George Bernard 7cr; Kevin Schafer 9; Laurie Campbell 25cl; Trevor McDonald 21cl. **Oxford Scientific Films:** 16tr, 20cr, 20l, 24crb, 28tr, 41tr; Bert & Babs Wells 17bl; Gordon Maclean 15b; Konrad Wothe 7tr; Michael Fogden 16bl; Robin Bush 17r; Satoshi Kuribayashi 20tl, 20cla, 20cl. **Science Photo Library:** Andrew Syred 12cb, 13br, 32cb; Astrid & Hanns-Frieder Michler 8bl; B.W Hoffmann/Agstock 6-7; Claude Nuridsany & Marie Perennou 14tr, 14ca, 16cl, 16clb, 33bl; Dan Suzio 3r; David Nunuk 37b; Dr Jeremy Burgess 34-35; Eye of Science 33cb; Gusto 10cl; James H. Robinson 15tl; Jan Hinsch 36c; John Durham 13br; PSU Entomology 15tr; Sinclair Stammers 35cb. **Still Pictures:** Markus Dlouhy 40l. **Zefa Visual Media:** Masterfile/R. Ian Lloyd 42bl.

All other images © Dorling Kindersley www.dkimages.com